FAST FACT MATH

FAST FACT MEASUREMENT

LINE CRAYON UP
WITH 0

4 INCHES
LONG

BY BLANCHE ROSSER

Gareth Stevens
PUBLISHING

Please visit our website, www.garethstevens.com. For a free color catalog of all our high-quality books, call toll free 1-800-542-2595 or fax 1-877-542-2596.

Cataloging-in-Publication Data

Names: Roesser, Blanche.
Title: Fast fact measurement / Blanche Roesser.
Description: New York : Gareth Stevens Publishing, 2019. | Series: Fast fact math | Includes index.
Identifiers: LCCN ISBN 9781538219850 (pbk.) | ISBN 9781538219836 (library bound) | ISBN 9781538219867 (6 pack)
Subjects: LCSH: Measurement–Juvenile literature.
Classification: LCC QA465.R64 2019 | DDC 530.8–dc23

First Edition

Published in 2019 by
Gareth Stevens Publishing
111 East 14th Street, Suite 349
New York, NY 10003

Copyright © 2019 Gareth Stevens Publishing

Designer: Sarah Liddell
Editor: Therese Shea

Photo credits: Cover, pp. 1, 12 (crayons) Studio DMM Photography, Designs & Art/Shutterstock.com; cover, p. 1 (ruler) Photo Melon/Shutterstock.com; chalkboard background used throughout mexrix/Shutterstock.com; p. 5 JeC Photography/Shutterstock.com; p. 7 (basketball hoop) rSnapshotPhotos/Shutterstock.com; p. 7 (soccer net) xjrshimada/Shutterstock.com; p. 7 (hockey puck) vkilikov/Shutterstock.com; p. 8 (top measuring tape) onair/Shutterstock.com; p. 8 (bottom measuring tape) Seregam/Shutterstock.com; pp. 8, 12 (rulers) Quang Ho/Shutterstock.com; p. 8 (meterstick) JMiks/Shutterstock.com; p. 8 (yardstick) John T Takai/Shutterstock.com; p. 9 (caterpillar) Marsha Mood/Shutterstock.com; p. 9 (basketball) taka1022/Shutterstock.com; p. 9 (kids) Kovalchuk Oleksandr/Shutterstock.com; p. 11 (giraffe) Justin Black/Shutterstock.com; p. 11 (tree) Gwoeii/Shutterstock.com; p. 13 (plant) Denisenko/Shutterstock.com; p. 13 (puppy) thanai asawaroengchai/Shutterstock.com; p. 13 (ruler) Frame Art/Shutterstock.com; p. 15 Devenorr/Shutterstock.com; p. 16 Hodyachaya Alla/Shutterstock.com; p. 17 JAYANNPO/Shutterstock.com; p. 19 Quality Stock Arts/Shutterstock.com; p. 21 Nick Barounis/Shutterstock.com.

Printed in the United States of America

CPSIA compliance information: Batch #CS18GS: For further information contact Gareth Stevens, New York, New York at 1-800-542-2595.

CONTENTS

Words in the glossary appear in **bold** type the first time they are used in the text.

WHY MEASURE?

Is measuring important? Without measuring, bridges might be too short, clothes might not fit, and your cookies might not taste right! Measuring is necessary in so many areas of life. From bakers to **engineers**, many people measure in their jobs every day.

There are many types of measurement, many measurement **units**, and many measurement tools. In this book, you'll learn some "fast facts" that will help you understand more about measurement in your world. Are you ready to become a master of measuring?

MATH MANIA!

As you read this book, you'll use your measurement skills to answer questions and **solve** problems in boxes like this. Look for the upside-down answers to check your work. Good luck!

4

MEASURING IS A KEY PART OF BAKING. OFTEN, YOU NEED TO ADD JUST THE RIGHT AMOUNT TO MAKE FOOD TASTE GOOD.

USEFUL UNITS

Americans often use standard units such as inches, feet, and miles. In other countries, people use metric units such as centimeters, meters, and kilometers.

For example, San Francisco and Los Angeles in California are about 380 miles, or 612 kilometers, apart. That's 24,080,000 inches, or 61,200,000 centimeters! Miles or kilometers provide a much easier number to deal with.

Use your knowledge of measurement units to answer the questions below:

a. Is a basketball hoop 10 feet high or 10 inches high?

b. Is a soccer goal $2\frac{1}{2}$ meters high or $2\frac{1}{2}$ centimeters high?

c. Is a hockey puck 3 feet across or 3 inches across?

Answer: a. 10 feet high, b. $2\frac{1}{2}$ meter high, c. 3 inches across

IT'S SMART TO KNOW ABOUT BOTH STANDARD AND METRIC UNITS. YOU'LL USE THEM BOTH IN LIFE.

THE TOOLS

Length, width, and height are often measured with units such as inches, feet, centimeters, and meters. Many rulers are only 12 inches (30 cm) long. If you want to measure a longer object, you could use a yardstick, meterstick, or measuring tape. Some measuring tapes are **flexible**, so they're helpful for measuring round or curved objects.

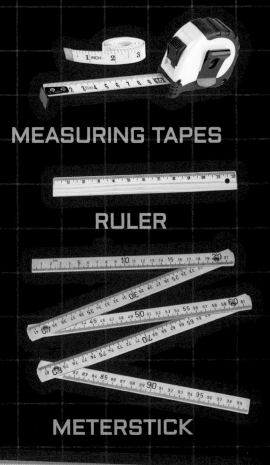

MEASURING TAPES

RULER

METERSTICK

YARDSTICK

MATH MANIA!

Answer each question below.

a. Which tool is best for measuring a caterpillar: a ruler or a yardstick?

b. Which tool is best for measuring around a basketball: a ruler or a measuring tape?

c. Which tool is best for measuring your height: a yardstick or a measuring tape?

Answer: a. a ruler, b. a measuring tape, c. a measuring tape

A YARDSTICK IS 3 FEET, OR 36 INCHES, LONG. A METERSTICK IS 1 METER, OR 100 CENTIMETERS, LONG. A MEASURING TAPE IS OFTEN LONGER THAN BOTH!

ESTIMATE IT!

You don't always have to use tools to measure. You can estimate using your knowledge of measurement units and the measurements of other objects.

For example, if you know your fork is about 8 inches long, you could estimate the width of a table. Imagine a table is 5 forks long. This **equation** could help you figure out how many inches long the table is:

$$8 \times 5 = ?$$

The table is about 40 inches long.

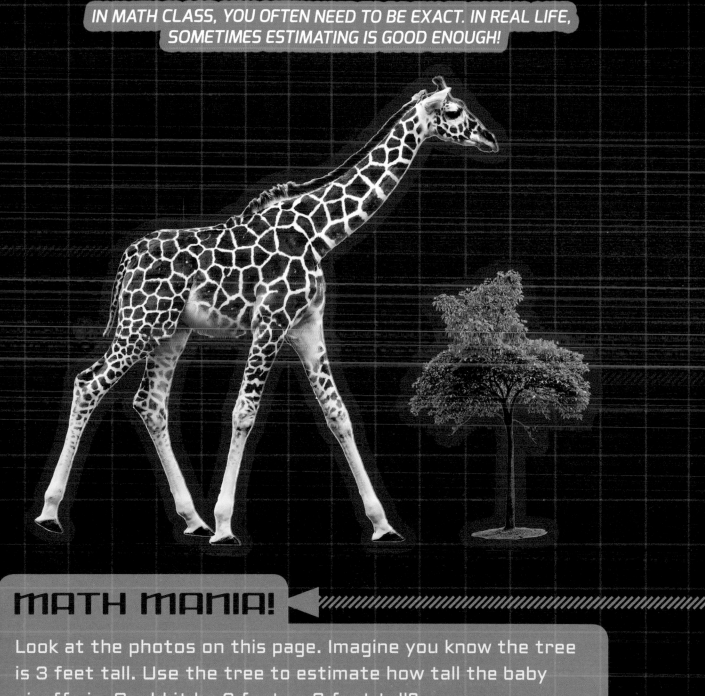

MATH MANIA!

Look at the photos on this page. Imagine you know the tree is 3 feet tall. Use the tree to estimate how tall the baby giraffe is. Could it be 3 feet or 6 feet tall?

Answer: 6 feet

PRACTICE MAKES PERFECT

In math class, your teacher may expect you to use different units and know about how big they are. Rulers often show inches on one side and centimeters on the other. This makes it easy to use both units and compare them. Let's practice with a ruler.

This crayon is 4 inches long. That's about 10 centimeters.

Measure the height of the puppy in the photo below using the ruler shown. About how many inches tall is it? About how many centimeters tall is it?

THIS PLANT IS ALMOST 2 INCHES TALL, WHICH IS ABOUT 5 CENTIMETERS.

Answer: The puppy is about 11 inches tall, or almost 28 centimeters.

VERY INTO VOLUME

Standard measurement units for liquid volume include cups, pints, and gallons. The metric units liters (L) and milliliters (ml) are most often used by scientists and in science classes. You might see both kinds of units labeled on foods and drinks sold in stores.

Measuring cups and **beakers** are tools that measure liquid volume. The sides of these containers are marked with lines. When you pour liquid into them, you can read the volume measurement of the liquid.

DID YOU KNOW THAT 500 MILLILITERS IS EQUAL TO $\frac{1}{2}$ LITER? YOU DO NOW!

MATH MANIA!

Solve the word problem about liquid volume below.

Dan has 18 liters of water. He **divides** the water equally among 6 beakers. How many liters does each beaker contain?

18 liters ÷ 6 beakers = ?

MEASURING MASS

We measure mass by weighing an object on a scale. In the United States, standard mass units include ounces and pounds. In other countries and often in science, the metric units grams and kilograms are used when measuring mass.

Scientists often use scales called balances to measure mass. These scales can be very exact, which is important for measuring matter used in experiments. Too much or too little of something can ruin results!

BALANCE

MATH MANIA! ◄ //

Solve the word problem about mass below.

Patrick collects rocks at the beach. All the rocks have the same mass. Patrick knows the mass of one rock is 20 grams.

What is the total mass of 5 rocks?

20 grams x 5 rocks = ?

TWO CONTAINERS THAT ARE THE SAME SIZE HAVE THE SAME VOLUME. HOWEVER, THEY MIGHT HAVE DIFFERENT MASSES IF THEY CONTAIN DIFFERENT MATERIALS!

IT'S ABOUT TIME

Time is another kind of measurement. You know that each hour is 60 minutes and each day is 24 hours. However, math problems about time can be tricky.

FAST FACT: Number lines can help you solve problems about time.

Imagine it's 8:30 a.m. You want to know how long it will be until lunch, which is served at 12:00 p.m. You can use a number line to find out.

30 MINUTES   3 HOURS

The number line helps you see that lunch is in $3\frac{1}{2}$ hours.

MATH MANIA!

Use the number line to answer the word problem below.

Peter will meet Violet at the park at 1 p.m. It is 9 a.m. now. How many hours until he meets her?

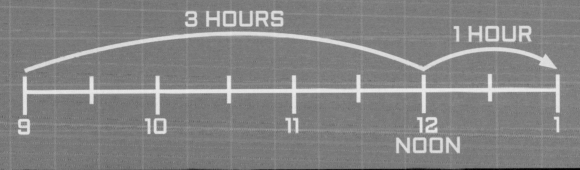

3 HOURS

1 HOUR

9   10   11   12   1
         NOON

YOU CAN USE NUMBER LINES TO HELP YOU SOLVE TIME PROBLEMS. SOON YOU'LL BE ABLE TO PICTURE THE NUMBER LINES IN YOUR HEAD!

MEASURING UP

There are many more kinds of measurement. Don't forget about **temperature**. You might check the outside temperature on a **thermometer** to know how to dress before you go out to play. Measuring really is a part of everyday life!

When you get older, you might choose a job in which measuring is important. Weather scientists, construction workers, and **architects** are just a few jobs in which it's necessary to measure exactly. Keep practicing your measuring, and you'll master it!

Use your knowledge of measurement units to match the unit on the left to the kind of measurement on the right:

a. milliliter   1. mass
b. feet   2. length
c. kilogram   3. volume
d. minute   4. time

Answer: a. 3, b. 2, c. 1, d. 4.

THERE'S A FAMOUS SAYING: MEASURE TWICE, CUT ONCE. THAT MEANS IT'S IMPORTANT TO DOUBLE-CHECK YOUR WORK SO YOU DON'T MAKE A MISTAKE!

GLOSSARY

architect: a person who plans buildings and gives advice about how they should be built

beaker: a wide glass with a lip for pouring that is used especially in science for holding and measuring liquids

container: an object that can hold something

divide: to separate into pieces or amounts

engineer: a person who plans and builds products, machines, systems, buildings, or other objects

equation: a statement in math that two values are equal

flexible: capable of bending or being bent

height: the measurement of how tall something is

solve: to find the correct answer for

temperature: how hot or how cold something is

thermometer: a tool for measuring temperature

unit: a particular amount of length, time, or other measurement that is used as a standard for counting or measuring

BOOKS

Dowdy, Penny. *Measurement.* New York, NY: Crabtree Publishing, 2009.

Sohn, Emily, and Karen J. Rothbardt. *Measurement: The Measured Mystery.* Chicago, IL. Norwood House Press, 2011.

Wingard-Nelson, Rebecca. *Math Measurement Word Problems: No Problem!* Berkeley Heights, NJ: Enslow Publishers, 2011.

WEBSITES

Measurement Index
www.mathsisfun.com/measure/index.html
Learn more about the two systems of measurement.

Third Grade Math: Units of Measurement
www.ixl.com/math/grade-3
Find lots of measuring practice in the links on this page.

INDEX